Bears

Written by
Jill Atkins

There are many different kinds of bear.

The biggest of all the bears is the **polar bear**.

Polar bears can be found on sea ice in the **Arctic**. They are strong swimmers in the icy water and they leap from ice floe to ice floe.

Polar bears spend a lot of time on land too, especially if they have cubs.

Polar bears hunt all year round and feed mainly on seals, but the Arctic Sea is slowly melting so their **habitat** is shrinking.

Polar bears sometimes need to go into towns to find food.

Fantastic fact

The polar bear looks white, but underneath the white fur its skin is black!

A polar bear cub

The **brown bear** is nearly as big as the polar bear.

Brown bears inhabit forests and mountains.

They often stand in a river and grab fish as the fish travel upstream.

The bears need a lot of patience to grab a fish. They must be quick too.

They are sometimes called **grizzly bears** because their brown fur is tinged with grey.

The adult bears cannot get up trees because they are too heavy.

Grizzly bears **hibernate** each winter and the cubs are born then. The cubs feed on their mum's milk.

Fantastic fact

When grizzly bears stand on their hind legs, they are much taller than the tallest man!

Black bears are much smaller than grizzly bears and they are lighter, so they are very quick at getting up trees.

They can run very fast too. They eat the same food as the grizzly and sleep through the winter.

There is danger if you meet a bear, especially if she is with her cubs. She will protect them and she might attack you.

So be sure to keep away from bears!

Fantastic fact

If black bears are hungry, they might go into town and hunt for food. So you need bear-proof rubbish bins!

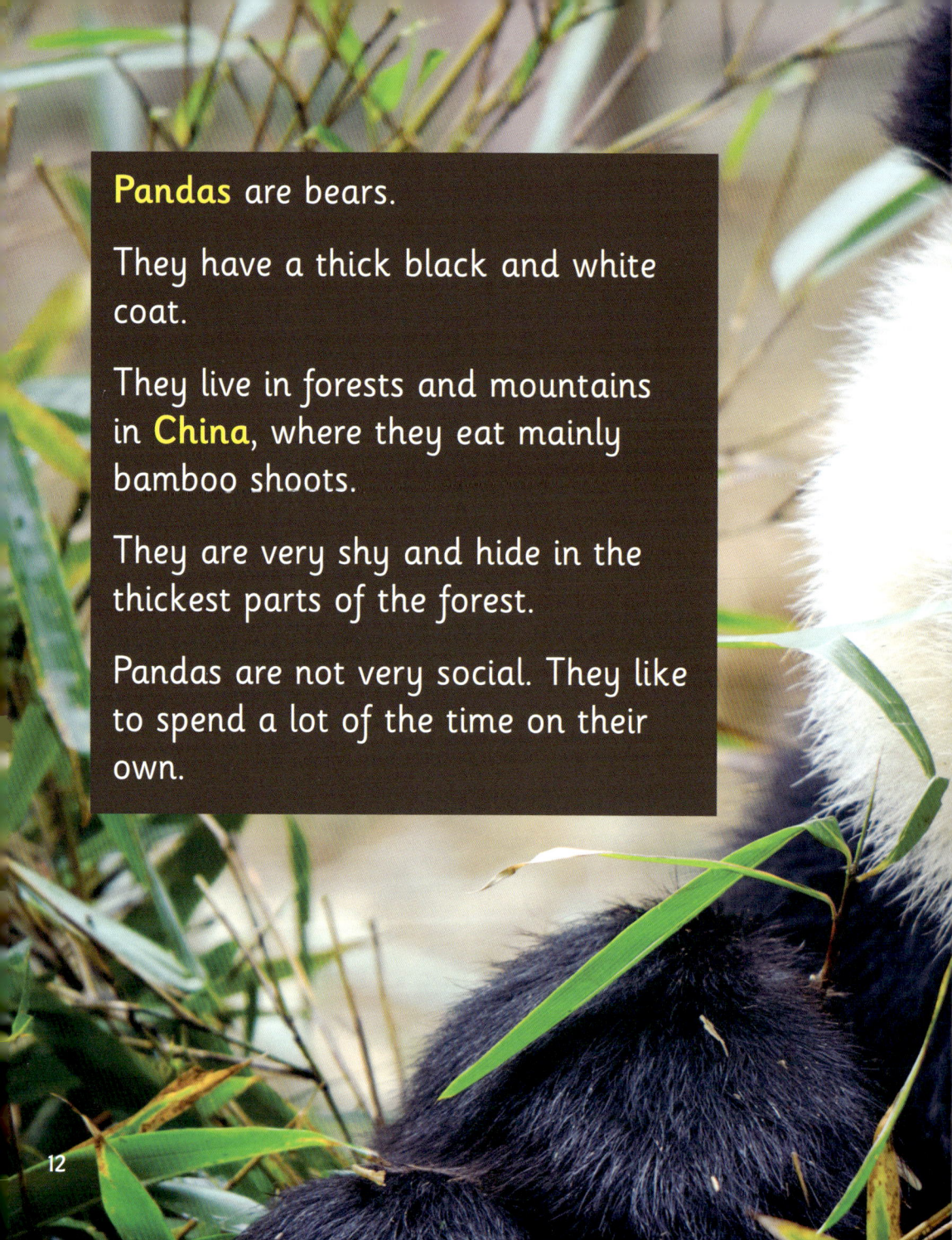

Pandas are bears.

They have a thick black and white coat.

They live in forests and mountains in **China**, where they eat mainly bamboo shoots.

They are very shy and hide in the thickest parts of the forest.

Pandas are not very social. They like to spend a lot of the time on their own.

Panda cubs are so tiny when they are born that some of them will die.

There are not many pandas left in the wild, but some can be found in zoos.

A panda cub

Fantastic fact

Pandas spend a lot of time sleeping, but they do not hibernate.

Some more kinds of bear:

Moon bear

Sun bear

Sloth bear

This is not a bear!

Have you got a bear?